The Senior Manager in School

THE ATTACHMENT AWARE SCHOOL SERIES
Bridging the gap for troubled pupils

ATTACHMENT AWARE SCHOOL SERIES

Bridging the gap for troubled pupils

Book 2

The Senior Manager
in School

Louise Michelle Bombèr

Worth Publishing

First published 2016 by Worth Publishing Ltd
worthpublishing.com

© Worth Publishing Ltd 2016

Printed and bound in Great Britain by TJ International,
Padstow, Cornwall

British Library Cataloguing in Publication Data
A catalogue record for this book is available from the British Library
ISBN   9781903269305

Cover and text design by Anna Murphy

For Jane Airey,
who played a significant role
in my journey

Biography

Louise Michelle Bombèr is a specialist Attachment Lead Teacher and a therapist. She has worked for many years with children and young people who have experienced significant relational traumas and losses. Working in many different contexts she is passionate about ensuring these pupils have opportunity to adapt and recover so that they can make the most of all that school offers. She continues to work as a practitioner using Theraplay, PACE, DDP and sensory interventions to support children and their parents.

Louise is the author of *Inside I'm Hurting*, *What About Me?*, co-author with Dr Dan Hughes of *Settling to Learn* and contributor to *Teenagers and Attachment*. Her work has been greatly influenced by John Bowlby, Dan Hughes, Daniel Siegel, Bruce Perry and Gabor Maté. Louise advises, trains and supports education professionals and families, and is involved in direct work with children and young people in class, in the therapy room and at an allotment project, PLOT 22. She heads up a network which enables Attachment Leads to be trained to provide advocacy and support in individual schools across the UK (attachmentleadnetwork.net).

Acknowledgements

Thanks to Dr Kim Golding for her continued partnership with me, and my long standing supervisor Penny Auton, who has walked alongside me in my professional journey over many, many years. I would like to thank Jenny Peters in the UK and Glen Cooper in the USA for generously providing me with commentary on Circle of Security®, which is such an invaluable resource to all those wanting to make a difference in children's lives.

I would like to honour all those Senior Managers who take time out of busy schedules every half-term in my support groups to reflect together on how best to truly include troubled children and adolescents. I know your work is challenging on many fronts, but thank you for truly affirming that education is for all.

My current TouchBase™ team - Jennie Fellows, Jessie Fuller, Julia Wilde, Keeley de Freese and Becs Uvieghara for your dedication and commitment to these children; it doesn't go unnoticed. My national trainers, Anne Henderson, Clare Langhorne and Alison

Lumley who so passionately deliver materials they believe in, whilst continuing as practitioners actively involved with many pupils. All the support assistants and mentors with whom I have journeyed since 2000; together we have learned what is needed.

My editor and friend Andrea Perry who encourages and mobilises me into further creativity. My husband Jonathan Fordham, who often releases me from household responsibilities because he believes in this cause as much as I do. Thanks for holding the fort when I bury my head in books and my laptop! Lucinda and Steve Smith who lead with both gentleness and strength, continuing to be really behind my vision to see dignity restored. Nothing goes unnoticed.

All the brave families who have endured more than many will ever know and yet remain standing clothed in dignity and strength and armed with fierce compassion for their hurting children. May this series of books play some part in raising much needed awareness so that you can take a step back, trusting the schools your children attend to nurture them into all they should have been first time around.

Foreword

This guide for senior managers helps us to understand the importance of leadership if schools are to be attachment organised rather than trauma organised. Whilst I was reading Louise's book and reflecting on her description of the role of the Senior Manager in an attachment aware and trauma informed school, I was impressed as always at the clarity of the guidance and her central focus on keeping the child in mind throughout the school day. It helped me to reflect on the pivotal role the Senior Manager has in facilitating this.

The way we are held in mind by others is an important part of discovering who we are. When secure children come into our schools, we have the comfort of knowing that these pupils are held in mind by their families. The child has developed a coherent, flexible sense of who he is and will be open to new experiences. The child (as pupil) is ready to learn. Louise, however, is focusing our attention on children who have not had this experience. In trauma organised families, parents struggle to hold the child in mind, and he or she in turn develops an incoherent, inflexible sense of self. He becomes closed to new experiences. The child is not ready to learn. The Senior Manager has a pivotal role in supporting the team to hold the child in mind. No one person can do this alone: but together, and with strong leadership, the child can get an experience that he deserved from birth and can begin to develop the emotional resilience that he needs to successfully move out into the world.

The **Attachment Aware Schools Series** is an important guide to all those within educational settings supporting children struggling with developmental trauma. The *Senior Manager in School* will be an important part of this, drawing, as does the whole series, on Louise's wealth of experience and understanding, translated into practical and supportive ideas. If the Senior Manager is to stay resilient and enabled to fulfil her supportive role, then she in turn will need support and guidance to draw upon. This book will be an important part of this support. All children deserve to be held in mind by those most closely living and working with them. The **Attachment Aware Schools Series** is a real contribution to ensuring that we all make this happen.

Kim S Golding 2016

Contents

continues/...

Please note: In this book I reference material from
my earlier publications, using acronyms for their titles for
accessibility. These books form a key resource for developing
attachment awareness and trauma informed interventions in
schools, and provide background reading for the **Attachment
Aware School Series.**

Inside I'm Hurting	(2009)	(**IIH**)
What About Me?	(2011)	(**WAM**)
Settling to Learn (with Dan Hughes)	(2013)	(**STL**)
Key Adult in School	(2015)	(**KAiS**)

Introduction

This pocket-sized book is part of the **Attachment Aware School Series**. The series has come about in response to an increasing understanding that security, through the experience of secure relationships, is necessary for every child to be able to settle to learn and make the most of all the educational opportunities out there. It is only when a child's **attachment system** is attended to that their **exploratory system** can really come into play.

Some children may have learned security outside school through their experience of relationships to date - others may not. Some pupils find settling into learning incredibly difficult, especially those who have a history of not being attended to, or responded to sufficiently, or often enough; of neglect, traumatic experience or significant loss. If circumstances have ruptured or inhibited the development of an internal, felt sense of security, then children often experience huge anxiety - sometimes unnoted by those of us observing.

The Senior Manager in School

These pupils are not in a position to learn or take up the huge range of opportunities available to them in school YET. So in school, we must first address their need for security and stability - by providing them with a consistent, reliable, empathic, attuned attachment relationship in school. Only then can we expect them to make progress with learning, and to fully engage with school life.

On really difficult days, even the most securely attached child - or adult - may find learning a struggle. So this series of pocket books endorses the view that if a school is fully attachment aware, *all children and staff will benefit.* Ideally all staff will have attachment aware training as their foundation, and with this background will appreciate that for some children a specific, targeted relational intervention will be a life-line.

In the **Attachment Aware School Series** we advocate having a small tight team around these specific pupils. So, in school we will have Team Lee, Team Grace, Team Aiden … four or five people in different positions of responsibility in the school. All believing *in* and rooting *for* the pupil.

> Having several good attachment relationships predicts better self-control, behaviour and relationships.
>
> Belsky et al 2007

In the primary phase, this team will usually be made up of the Key Adult, a back-up adult if appropriate, the class teacher, and a **Senior Manager** (SENCO or INCO, the Assistant Head or the Head). In the secondary phase, this would usually be the Key Adult, the form tutor, a subject teacher (*see* p.27), and one or two **Senior Managers** (the Head of Year, the SENCO/INCO and the Assistant Head). In addition to this school-based team, each pupil needs to know that their parents or carers are on board in their education, trusting those involved to support their child and actively working in tight partnership within their unique team.

With this in mind, there are five books in the **Attachment Aware School Series**, each reflecting the different roles of the different individuals in the team around the pupil (one pocket book for each member of the team). The series is written to help this valuable community work well together and hold the pupil in mind, shoring the pupil up when necessary, serving as an anchor so that anxieties can be relieved; freeing up the possibility for this child or young person to become all they were intended to become, first time around. I have also included a pocket book for the parents or carers of the child or young person, since they will be and often are valuable contributors to the school team.

Throughout each book you'll find some key terms are highlighted in **bold**: you'll find all of these in the **Glossary** on p.81.

The Senior Manager in School

This particular book is intended for those who have been identified as the **Senior Manager** responsible for a particular troubled pupil as part of Team Pupil.

Senior Managers have a significant role in Team Pupil. They have both a personal and strategic function. The pupil will experience safety knowing there is someone in such a responsible position within their team and having the opportunity to build a positive, close relationship with him or her. However, as well as knowing the pupil on an individual basis, the **Senior Manager** is also well placed to create interest in the school around attachment awareness and trauma informed interventions, to facilitate opportunities for training, and for organising continuing professional development to maintain the momentum.

Senior Managers are usually well respected professionals within the school community, and so modelling appropriate ways of being and relating around this pupil will be important for the rest of Team Pupil. It will be the **Senior Manager's** role to select appropriate Teaching Assistants or mentors to be allocated to these troubled pupils, working towards the best match. To fully understand the role and responsibilities of the Key Adult, please read the pocket book intended for those taking that role (**Attachment Aware School Series** Book 1, *Key Adult in School* (*given here as* **KAiS**)).

The **Senior Manager** will be responsible for re-grouping

Team Pupil to meet with the assigned pupil on a regular basis to remind the pupil they are being 'kept in mind,' and also to ensure that professional network meetings are convened as and when necessary. The **Senior Manager** needs to be clear about limits within the support work, and know the different external professionals outside the school context who can be referred to if necessary.

The **Senior Manager** takes on a Key Adult type role with the Teaching Assistant or mentor allocated, checking in on them so they feel 'held in mind' too: supporting and encouraging them, and ensuring that all the support work taking place is honouring the developmental pace of the pupil. Not so slow that the pupil remains stuck, and not so fast that the pupil becomes overwhelmed. The **Senior Manager** is responsible for the correct processes being in place to ensure this pupil receives the most appropriate level of support to enable them to reach their potential within the school context.

Whilst the Key Adult has the closest relationship with the parents and carers of the troubled pupil, the **Senior Manager** will become more directly involved if there are any significant successes or concerns.

Key Adults are usually members of support staff - teaching assistants (TAs), individual needs assistants (INAs), emotional literacy support assistants (ELSAs) or mentors from the main school staff within a school. Key Adults prepare themselves to be the best **additional attachment figures** they can be for those pupils who have experienced toxic stress from pregnancy onwards, and/or have had compromised or **disrupted relationships/connections** with adults in their early years.

We now know that a history of **relational trauma and loss** needn't be a life sentence of insecure attachments, **developmental vulnerabilities**, low educational outcomes and a compromised future. Children and young people *can* learn security and can negotiate and consolidate the necessary developmental milestones: but they need us all alongside them to do so.

Education from 5 to 16 is compulsory in the UK, and so these children and young people will be with us for many weeks, terms and years. If they have been wounded '*within relationship*,' it makes sense for us to prioritise and use quality relational interventions to help them, as *relationship* is the necessary vehicle for supporting adaption and recovery.

> For many children and young people, a sense of connectedness with just one adult … is enough to end their deep sense of aloneness, isolation, not belonging, not being understood.
>
> Sunderland 2015, p.19

We know now that both emotional growth and well-being

are directly linked to learning. We also know that the more a child or young person experiences quality connections with mature adults, the more mature his brain becomes.

So it is the **Senior Manager's** strategic role to ensure that time and resources are invested into facilitating relationally rich contexts for this particular group of pupils with challenging histories of **relational trauma** and loss. A priority will be to invest in people, so there are more adults in the school who are aiming to be attachment aware and trauma informed in their interventions with pupils.

We also know from neuroscience that the richer *relational experiences* these pupils have, the more complex the neural pathways and connections in their brains will be, meaning that relationships bring integration. Integration brings health - physical, mental and emotional health. And richer relational experiences and more complex systems in the brain mean the pupil will be able to engage in more complex thinking, relating and being. This is the way ahead for all of us who take our pupils' well-being and development seriously. **Senior Managers** are well placed to take the lead in making this happen.

> Let's shift from a behavioural view of pupils to a relational one - focussing on trying to understand what their behaviour means [or communicates].
> Hughes & Baylin 2012, p.8 (*my parantheses*)

The Senior Manager in School

Up until recently, it was thought that the responsibility to support the mental health and well-being of these children and young people lay solely with their parents/carers, social workers and therapists. However, I know first-hand from many years of experience out in schools how powerful a Key Adult relationship and an assigned pupil team can be within the educational context.

Key Adults who are physically and emotionally present, attentive, attuned and responsive, provide the ground for these children and young people to thrive. And those Key Adults who also employ *playfulness*, communicate *acceptance*, engage *curiosity* and show *empathy* (Hughes, 2009, *and see* Book 1, *in this series*, **KAiS**) can actually support these children and young people into new learning, development and opportunities. The possibilities are endless!

I also know of the huge difference it makes to a pupil, to a teacher, to a class, to a whole school community if **Senior Managers** are actively involved in attachment aware and trauma informed interventions. Sadly I also know of many cases where **Senior Managers** were not onside, and this has led to school placement breakdowns. This is how significant a **Senior Manager's** role is, for better or for worse.

Teacher-student attunement is not a 'nice addition' to the learning experience but a core requirement.

Cozolino 2013, p.18

To make the best use of this book, your whole school community would first ideally have had at least two full days of training in child development, attachment and neuroscience, to create a platform for effective, consistent, attachment aware practice in school. All these key principles and practices will obviously need to be re-visited on a regular basis in order to truly embed the work I'll be outlining in this book (and throughout the **Attachment Aware Schools Series**) into the usual ways of how we are and what we do within the school culture.

In addition, I recommend that each school allocates an interested member of support staff and Senior Management to train up as **Attachment Leads** so that they can ensure quality practice, and keep the momentum going (*see* attachmentleadnetwork.net).

A NOTE ABOUT CONSULTATION

Each of us needs to be clear as to the boundaries of our role and responsibilities. There are occasions when attachment aware interventions will not be sufficient, and a trauma informed practitioner will need to be involved for specialist assessments, advice and interventions.

Who should that individual be? I would strongly recommend a specialist therapist with complex trauma/developmental trauma expertise. Our children and young people need appropriate professionals involved who will provide an extension to the ground work already laid down within the attachment aware practices employed by a school. This is our joint ethical responsibility. As well as detailed assessments and direct interventions, these same professionals can also provide specialist supervision to staff in school on a regular basis. Increasing staff care increases our care-giving capacity, which means that we will then be more able to facilitate the permanency that our pupils need. By facilitating and honouring the vehicle of relationship, we will be 'respecting biology' (Perry, 2014).

It is the **Senior Manager's** role to lead on all this by overviewing the work going on in school and making the judgement call as to when and if external consultation might be needed. It is helpful when **Senior Managers** link up with others in nearby schools to determine where their teams might receive the best types of support. In Brighton & Hove, for example, I run support groups for each member of Team Pupil on a half-termly basis. Perhaps different authorities might run similar groups (*and see* p.69)?

Part One

Becoming an attachment aware Senior Manager

The aim of this book

This book supports **Senior Managers** to be the best leaders they can be in this specialist area of attachment aware support in schools. Troubled pupils require much thought, reflection and skill. It is essential that those taking up strategic positions, especially within Team Pupil, do not take this responsibility lightly, but view it as an amazing opportunity to further inclusion in both policy and practice in unchartered territories within school. There will be many times when a **Senior Manager** may experience some isolation, as attachment awareness and trauma informed interventions still remain relatively new in many schools up and down the UK. This book will therefore help the **Senior Manager** to remain focussed and single-minded, despite the obstacles that will inevitably appear.

The Senior Manager in School

What does a Senior Manager in the attachment aware context do, and why?

The **Senior Manager** takes the lead in the formation and growth of Team Pupil, the team around a troubled pupil. Responsibilities will vary from making a good match of Key Adult to pupil, through to freeing up staff to spend quality time with pupils in their care, to advocacy in the wider school community. The role of the **Senior Manager** is varied, meaning a range of skills is necessary.

The troubled pupil needs to experience the **Senior Manager** as 'big' enough, wise enough, kind enough and strong enough to 'hold them' psychologically (Circle of Security®, *see* p.22, *and* **Glossary**.). So it is important that the **Senior Manager** is comfortable in his or her own skin and is not fazed by the rollercoaster ride that can come as a result of getting close to trauma. Someone who is secure enough not to engage in power dynamics within school. Someone who is able to laugh playfully!

These particular pupils have often had an overdose of power, authority and control being used to their detriment, by those who we would have hoped would have provided sensitive, attuned care to their needs. They will be expecting more of the same from other grown-ups they meet. The **Senior Manager** needs to facilitate different kinds of experiences for these pupils. With the support of a team - Team Pupil - the **Senior Manager** sets out to 'tame' the troubled pupil who has experienced intimacy betrayal of all sorts, to begin to trust the grown-ups in the context of school.

I believe that **Senior Managers** are best placed to reclaim the word 'discipline' in school, as Daniel Siegel (2015, p.xiv) describes (*and see* p.55). It seems that many people have not realised that discipline is actually about learning through instruction, and not about punishment. As discipline is really all about learning, the **Senior Manager** can set the tone and pace of how and when that learning takes place. Learning is severely compromised when troubled pupils are in a state of alarm, fear or terror. However, when they are in a state of calm or calm alert, and they experience connection first (*and see* p.56), why would they not be able to digest what we are saying?

Senior Managers can only lead by example, and it is important that they remember that staff and pupils are watching their every move. It is therefore critical that they stay ahead of the game! It would be advisable for the **Senior Manager** to be clear about all the roles and responsibilities of those around a troubled pupil in school, so that boundaries can be clear, not blurred. One way to assist in this is to read the whole **Attachment Aware Schools Series**. It would also be beneficial for the **Senior Manager** to upskill themselves by reading around this area, for example *Inside I'm Hurting* (2009), (**IIH**), *What About Me?* (2011), (**WAM**), and with Dan Hughes, *Settling to Learn* (2013), (**STL**) (*please see* p.xii).

The Senior Manager in School

Ideal qualities of a Senior Manager

Aspiring to be the best Senior Manager for these pupils

Willing to take an ethical stand in response to questioning

Regulated ☆ Strategic ☆ Assertive ☆ Pioneering

Secure in one's own identity as these pupils will challenge your capabilities

Taking the lead ☆ Provider of relentless care

Robust enough to manage not only the pupil's intense feelings but the feelings of Team Pupil too!

Containing ☆ Kind ☆ Flexible thinker ☆ Hopeful

Personable - able to relate to pupils, Team Pupil, external professionals and parents/carers

Nurturing ☆ Playful ☆ Wise ☆ Creative

Efficient - able to take things forward in a timely way

Moral conscience ☆ Grounded ☆ Patient ☆ Calm

Willing to stand out from the crowd - not everyone is school will agree with your decisions

Facilitative ☆ Accepting ☆ Curious ☆ Empathic

Passionate about inclusion on every level

Being a strong advocate - not everyone will want this troubled pupil in your school

Able to take responsibility and apologise if necessary to both the pupil and Team Pupil

Core aims of the Senior Manager

The Senior Manager's aims are to

1   ensure that all staff have sufficient training and access to resources and support in order for them to use attachment awareness and trauma informed interventions within their everyday practice

2   keep trauma on the agenda so that it is not overlooked in the busy-ness and ever changing demands of school life

3   monitor all school policies and practices to ensure they are *enabling* pupils who have experienced relational trauma and loss, not *disabling* them

4   select appropriate support staff to take on the important role of Key Adult in school for individual pupils, through assessment and interview to ensure good matches

The Senior Manager in School

5 free up staff to meet with pupils in their
care regularly, to liaise with one another
and to receive appropriate supervision
and support

6 include Key Adults in all meetings about
their assigned troubled pupil: enable them
to be honoured and to have a strong
voice in decision-making

7 liaise with external agencies to provide
effective and appropriate consultation

Good questions about attachment aware Senior Managers

⤷ *Does this mean Senior Managers need to be therapists now too?*

No, definitely not! You are teachers. But it would be foolish to overlook therapeutic principles and practices which are known to be helpful in other contexts when attempting to support troubled pupils to settle to learn. We need as many tools as possible. We don't want to exacerbate problems out of pure ignorance. There is so much we can do to make a difference before we need to call in the trauma experts, but they will be needed from time to time! Let's not work in isolation.

⤷ *Does this mean Senior Managers need to start using support staff differently?*

Yes, definitely! Our current systems of identifying and allocating support staff are antiquated. Isn't it time to update and encourage specialisms based on experience, skill and interest? I would love to see Key Adults as a new protected role within schools. Now is the time.

⤷ *Does this mean I'm not going to be able to be organised and set times for all my support staff on my provision map?*

I'd recommend that you continue doing that for curriculum support and interventions groups. However, for troubled pupils an element of flexibility is required, or what I call flexi-support. All interventions need to be state dependent (that is, responsive to the state of the pupil) and because their states shift throughout any given day, our support needs to shift too. If we don't have flexibility built in, then we will inevitably run into difficulties.

↳ *Does this mean we are going to need more budget?*

Sometimes, yes, we will need to advocate for more on behalf of vulnerable pupils. We know that these pupils will do much better if we increase human contact for our pupils. I have been told by **Senior Managers** that they have seen significant shifts in all areas of school life when scarce resources are invested into people hours.

However, most of the time you will find that shifting the *emphasis* of your existing support staff will make a considerable difference too. Don't be afraid to rock the boat! The child or young person needs to be at the centre of all interventions.

And when they are settled into learning, through the secure attachment relationship their Key Adult and Team Pupil provide, that will save you money elsewhere, in terms of less breakages, less disrupted time in class and lower staff turnover. And better learning for all in more peaceful classrooms. Big claims! But this is what **Senior Managers** report from schools where attachment aware and trauma informed principles and practice are embedded.

Part Two

The attachment aware Senior Manager in Team Pupil

Within an overall attachment aware school policy, your role is strategic. You will be the one who identifies those pupils who need a Key Adult. I strongly recommend that you do this for all pupils who have experienced significant **relational traumas** and losses (viewed as at risk, vulnerable, a cause for concern, in care, adopted, special guardianships) in their early years and are compromised in some area of their life at either home or school, or both. It is essential that we identify and work alongside these pupils sooner rather than later, both as a preventative measure and because we know from neuroscience that brain growth/organisation/re-organisation happens at a faster rate earlier in one's life.

The Senior Manager in School

We now have an ethical responsibility to act swiftly, especially knowing from research that these pupils are severely compromised as compared to their peers in the classroom.

Key functions of the Senior Manager within Team Pupil

I   ALLOCATING HOURS

Ensure the right Key Adult (and back-up adult if necessary) is allocated for the right number of hours (to assist you to choose the most appropriate member of support staff for this significant role, do read (**IIH**) and the first book in this series, (**KAiS**). Please see the list of ideal qualities of a Key Adult on p.12 of (**KAiS**): some schools are creating their person specifications for this role on the basis of this. You are likely to need to experiment with the number of hours of support. The minimum would be a half hour withdrawal session per week of quality 1:1 undivided attention away from others, and the maximum would be 25 hours, a mix of in-class and withdrawal time. How you go about deciding this, in discussion with Team Pupil, will be based on the level of structure and supervision you feel the pupil requires at this time, determined by both their developmental vulnerabilities and needs and the level of risk around both for themselves and others they come into contact with. In fact there is a very small minority of pupils who will need a period of stabilisation outside class before they are ready to learn, or even be in a position to integrate with other pupils (extending the safe space concept, see *Settling to Learn* (**STL,** p.38). Remember that investing more to begin with will give excellent returns over time, and that it is easier to reduce time than to increase it.

2 CO-ORDINATING AND FACILITATING TEAM PUPIL

Together with the Key Adult you write the initial Factfile (*see* **STL**) and set up the home/school partnership (*see* **WAM**). Part of your role will also to be to ensure the pupil has an initial Individual Development Plan (*see* **STL**). When the work begins between the Key Adult and the pupil, your role will be to build in regular reviews and determine whether sufficient progress is being made. Please note that the profiles of troubled pupils are not usually sequential or progressive, but spikey! (Ofsted please note! *and see* p.24). Watch out for the highs but be prepared for the lows. It may be necessary to re-visit earlier strategies previously used when there is any kind of regression. It may also be necessary for a trauma specialist to come in and carry out a more detailed assessment from a **developmental trauma** perspective, and write up an IDP for 2-3 years for Team Pupil to follow. The Seguridad model is recommended (*see* p.54).

3 MONITORING PROGRESS

Keep an eye on the overall states of the pupil, their emotional and social age and their recovery times from low level stressors in the school context. You ask the questions and hold Team Pupil accountable for what is going on in the process. Are they using the plan? Are they noticing changes? Are they identifying stressors and calmers?

4   IDENTIFYING PUPIL NEEDS

The **Circle of Security**® (*see* **Useful Contacts** *and* **Glossary**) helps us to understand that we need to identify where our troubled pupils are on the circle.**   Your work as a **Senior Manager** is to help the staff around you to attune to the needs of our pupils. Right now, does our pupil need close proximity to support her nurture needs, or is she ready to go out with our encouragement and support? Or does she need strong **containment** from you, so she can feel psychologically held? For more information on containing and holding children psychologically, *see* Greenlagh (1994). Skill is needed, as pupils who have been wounded within relationship have become very good at hiding what they really need but it doesn't mean we shouldn't attend to them.

5   SUPPORTING THE KEY ADULT
AND TEAM PUPIL

Ensuring Team Pupil is getting enough support and space to share, reflect on and process their experience of working with the Key Pupil is crucial. Especially for the Key Adult, your consistent, empathic, attuned support will be essential if he or she is going to be able to do this challenging work well. He or she needs to know they can turn to you, share successes and doubts, ask for your input and let you know when they have reached their limits. It is essential that you use what psychologist Dan Hughes (2009) has named PACE (playfulness, acceptance, curiosity, empathy) within all your interactions with staff and pupils (*see* **KAiS** p.73). Keep in mind that acceptance enables and so your member of the support staff will extend themselves further if they feel this from you. Evaluation disables, and this will hamper productivity (*see* **STL** *for more detail on PACE and communicating acceptance*). Staff care and your staff's care-giving capacity are directly correlated (*see* p.72). So if your Key Adult feels supported, not only will you hold onto good staff for longer but the pupils they are working with will experience permanency of relationship, as well - a pre-cursor for adaption and recovery.

6   ATTACHMENT AWARENESS FOR ALL

Your role also includes ensuring the whole school community is trained up in attachment awareness and trauma informed interventions by those education practitioners who are experienced and qualified in supporting pupils suffering from experiences of **relational traumas** and losses. Make sure everyone's training is topped up on a regular basis. and that up-to-date resources are available to all staff to enable them to be the best they can be. Make sure also that the rest

The **Circle of Security® *is a relationship-based early intervention programme designed to enhance attachment security between parents and children, and includes useful graphics for those involved with children to get a sense of a child's needs at any one time. (and see* **Glossary***)*

of the staff team understands their role in supporting Team Pupil, and be responsive to any challenges to this.

7 LIAISING WITH PARENTS AND CARERS

It is the Key Adult's responsibility to complete the home/ school partnership prompt sheets each week, to build the relationship with the family. However, as **Senior Manager**, you will be the first person to introduce the support work and to hold responsibility for Team Pupil, and so it makes sense for some kind of face-to-face introduction for the parents. If there are any significant changes for better or worse, it would be appropriate for you to step in again, but always in partnership with the Key Adult.

8 LIAISING WITH OUTSIDE AGENCIES, INCLUDING OFSTED

It is the **Senior Manager's** role to determine as and when other agencies need to be involved to support the pupil's adaption and recovery. However, it's really important that the Key Adult takes the lead in 'how' any recommendations are integrated in the support work - otherwise the relationship with the assigned pupil and the existing support work can easily be undermined, and there is a serious risk of increasing fragmentation for the pupil who is often already fragmented due to the impact of trauma. All our work needs to be integrated. Remember to create smaller worlds for the pupil in terms of limited transitions and the number of people involved with them.

In terms of Ofsted, it is essential that the processes you are using from an attachment aware perspective are highlighted, and that opportunities are maximised to educate inspectors around the spikey profiles these particular troubled pupils have. Pupils who have experienced significant **relational traumas** and losses do not have linear outcomes and progress charts: this is not linked to 'teacher performance', but to the erratic (and traumatic!) nature of trauma! Case studies are known to really support this understanding. Please note that there is work going on by the Consortium for Emotional Wellbeing in Schools and IRCT (Institute of Recovery from Childhood Trauma) to ensure all those involved with these pupils have a greater understanding (*see* **Useful Contacts**, p.97).

9   RESOURCING AND ALLOCATING FINANCE

It is the **Senior Manager's** role to lead on identifying the resources needed and then allocating the appropriate funding. Sometimes this will involve advocacy. A school seeking to be attachment aware and trauma informed in its approaches and interventions will invest its money - however scarce - into staffing and contact hours. Then it will allocate funding into facilitating and enabling space within school for sensory comfort. At the moment in the UK there are different budgets that can be used for these purposes - pupil premium, pupil premium plus and the Adoption Support Fund. Remember, however, to use every opportunity to raise the profile of these pupils with your Head and governors so that there is a general fund allocation too. Remember that attachment aware practices will benefit the whole school community. And let's also remember that for troubled pupils, these practices will be a lifeline.

10 UPSKILLING YOURSELF!

To enable you to extend your knowledge and skills in this entire area of expertise in school, I would strongly recommend that you and one of your Key Adults attend a seven day intensive course for **Attachment Leads**: this way you can deepen your understanding further and truly lead others into different ways of relating from an in-depth attachment aware and trauma informed perspective (please visit www.attachmentleadnetwork.net).

Responsibilities of Senior Managers

▷ Match financial resources to 'face to face time' for troubled pupils, with regular, permanent staff in the school

▷ Identify which of your staff would be most appropriately matched to troubled pupils, taking up the role of Key Adult. Play to their individual strengths. Not all staff are suitable (*see Key Adult in School* (**KAiS**), **Attachment Aware School Series,** Book 1, p.12)

▷ Identify which Key Adults would be best matched to particular pupils with:

a) some kind of relational disruption *or*

b) some kind of compromised presentation either at school *or* home *or* both

▷ For high profile children, ensure there is a back-up adult allocated too, so that there is a level of flexibility built in for the 'unexpected'. In secondary, I recommend choosing a subject teacher for Team Pupil from an area in which the Key Pupil has shown aptitude, interest or particular gifts. Please be aware that even though some of your pupils may be compliant in the school context, they will still need an allocated Key Adult *(see note below concerning some of our avoidant or avoidant/disorganised pupils, p.33)*.

The Senior Manager in School

▷ Organise a varied caseload for each Key Adult.
For example, it would not be appropriate to give
one Key Adult all the reactive or disorganised
pupils to work with.

▷ Prepare your Key Adult emotionally by
reminding them of the likely rollercoaster
nature of this work. For example, they may feel
deskilled at times, they may get rejected, they
may feel they are not making an impact ... these
feelings are all *natural* when working alongside
someone who has experienced **relational
trauma** and loss, as there is so much going on
in the unconscious that is very powerful. Key
Adults may also get tangled up in the pupil's
past, as these pupils can get very mixed up
between the past and the present. Your role is
to help them recognise and reflect on this.

▷ Ensure Team Pupil know who they all are!
Take a photo of them together. Introduce them
to the pupil together. Encourage them all to be
explicit with the pupil about what they are up
to: *"to support you to feel safe and comfortable
in our school, to enable you to make the most of
every opportunity here"* in appropriate language
determined by the pupil's emotional and social
age.

▷ Ensure other members of staff understand and
respect the role of the Key Adult.

▷ Ensure your Key Adults are connected in with other Key Adults from other schools. The best and easiest way to do this is by facilitating support groups for them, preferably off-site, to encourage a protected reflective space. I would strongly recommend that **Attachment Leads** or others who are trauma informed facilitate these (and ensure the facilitators receive supervision too!).

▷ Enable supervision for Key Adults with someone trained up therapeutically, whether this be in the context of 1:1 or in a group. A good rule of thumb is around once every half-term when supporting a pupil with an avoidant attachment presentation: once every three weeks for those supporting a pupil with an ambivalent attachment presentation, and once a week/fortnightly for those supporting a pupil with a disorganised/ reactive attachment presentation (Geddes 2006).

▷ Create a Factfile together with the Key Adult for this pupil.

▷ Start building connections with the wider team outside school. (see (**WAM**), p.273)

▷ Encourage meaningful weekly home/school contact whatever the school phase, using the prompt sheets outlined in (**STL**) (p.348). This will mean protecting non-contact time for your Key Adult on a Friday afternoon, and ensuring they have had opportunity to access and read the parent/carer's prompt sheet sometime on Monday morning.

▷ Create an Individual Development Plan for a pupil (see **(STL)** p.346). Please note that this must be created and followed at the beginning to check out the pupil's responses.

▷ If a pupil and/or Key Adult become 'stuck' at some point, refer out to a mental health professional who is not only attachment aware but trauma informed for an in-depth assessment and their specialised recommendations (a longer, more in-depth IDP.

▷ Encourage your Key Adults to use the IDP as a working document. I encourage Key Adults to use highlighters to show what they are currently working on.

▷ If possible, become the Key Adult to your chosen Key Adults. By this I mean, build protected time into your timetable to check in with your Key Adults. The time invested in staff care will save money in the long run.

▷ When you meet up with the Key Adult, check how they are, using PACE (Hughes 2009) (see p.23): managing their own stress which the work will have invariably caused, how they are holding their boundaries and what their hopes for their pupil are, for the next developmental phase.

▷ Do encourage your Key Adults as you go along. Draw attention to the Key Adult's strengths, especially what they are contributing towards their pupil's wellbeing.

▷ When there are difficulties for and with the pupil, as there may well be, ensure you first refer to the Key Adult before getting too involved. Ensure they contribute to any plans and that they are in agreement. After all, they will become the expert on the pupil in the school context. That is one of their key roles.

▷ Ensure the wider school community always delay their responses to any difficulties by referring first to the Key Adult, and then Team Pupil as and when appropriate.

▷ Invite your Key Adults to all meetings about the pupil, whatever the level of importance. They need to be there, as they will represent the voice of the pupil as well as be a great advocate. Unfortunately I have experienced Key Adults being overlooked, bypassed and even having information withheld from them. Some senior staff think they are protecting their staff in some way, when actually this is very risky practice that undermines the valuable work they are involved in. This kind of support work requires Key Adults to share something of themselves with these pupils, and that implies vulnerability. We need to ensure that the relationship between the Key Adult and the pupil always remains our core focus. It requires attention and protection. Let's protect what we know about this key vehicle towards adaption and recovery.

▷ Create your own Book of Success on troubled pupils. Note anything that Team Pupil notices and identifies as evidence of healthy or appropriate ways of being. It is so easy to dwell on the difficulties and negatives. We need to work at keeping our hope alive on behalf of these pupils.

▷ Create an attachment awareness/trauma informed policy for your school based on at least two days of training for the whole school community and through background reading. Helpful resources can be found on www.theyellowkite.co.uk called Atttachment Aware Schools. The whole school community needs to be on board, and it is your role to support and maintain that ongoing focus.

Remember attachment awareness is not 'the next big thing' to be replaced next year by something else. Attachment awareness is for life! Our primary work is to teach children, not subjects. Relationship and security are at the heart of children's ability to settle to learn, not bolt-on 'useful but not essential' extras. Be the one who holds this vision for these children, for your staff and for your whole school; and then watch how your pupils fly and make great progress, and your staff want to stay in post and gain so much more satisfaction from their work. Your pupils' parents will be happier too. Everybody is a winner.

A NOTE ABOUT AVOIDANT PRESENTATION

In the past, in my experience, many schools have made the mistake of overlooking those pupils with backgrounds of **relational trauma** and loss who are quiet and compliant, assuming they are 'OK'. They are not. Remember that when working in an attachment aware and trauma informed way, we must focus on 'hidden' needs, not just on what is 'presented'.

These pupils can be 'in hiding', and often have very disrupted stress response systems, and actually be struggling with high levels of anxiety. In fact if we were to measure their cortisol levels (the stress hormone) they would be very dysregulated in response to what we might call 'low level' stressors. Things are not always the way they seem. Often such pupils can 'hold it together' at school and then fall apart at home, and not because their parents or carers need parenting classes (*see* p.46).

So let's be pro-active, and allocate a Key Adult to these pupils too, ensuring the Key Adult has an active role in supporting them - even if they don't 'look like' they need support.

The Senior Manager in School

10 things Key Adults say about attachment

They help you keep going as they understand the work and 'get' the pupil.

With the right kind of attachment aware context even Team Pupil starts to flourish.

They respect our views and actually make decisions informed by our reflections.

School life is busy but those Senior Managers that take the time to listen make you feel so valued.

I now feel that I have so much to offer this pupil, and I'm sure it's because my Senior Manager has believed in me and the process, rather than feeling like someone is trying to catch me out.

aware Senior Managers:

The pupil I work with now feels like he belongs! He used to say he was not noticed. He knows he is now.

It makes school life so much easier when your Senior Manager is determined to see consistency.

Respect breeds respect. I know I have more to give to even those pupils that are reactive because I've been respected.

Having a good Senior Manager means that we can create a smaller world for a pupil who needs to feel secure.

They involve all of us as we all have an important part to play.

The Senior Manager in School

Part Three

Attachment awareness and trauma informed practice in schools

As a **Senior Manager** you are well placed to facilitate an attachment aware and trauma informed school culture. Here I outline five key areas I believe form the foundation of best practice: the ethos, the school environment, policy and practice, how to keep the momentum going, and facilitating staff care. All these factors will create a school that attracts and retains the right kind of staff, who will be able to engage in the most helpful interventions for pupils who are hurting. Your school will also be able to include these children for longer, as they will experience feeling physically and psychologically 'held'.

A THE ETHOS

In order to create the most helpful school context for troubled children the following aspects of the school ethos need to be considered. I've highlighted the ones that I think are the most significant, but obviously there are many others!

1   Create golden expectations for staff
2   Increase relational contact
3   Be well
4   Be both attachment aware *and* trauma informed
5   Enable the pupil
6   Include the anxious parent

1 Create golden expectations for staff

On the intensive courses I run, I always ask staff to come up with their 'golden principles' for the whole school staff team, to ensure, from an attachment aware and trauma focussed perspective, that the school ethos and all interactions and communications with troubled pupils are respectful and instil dignity.

Our troubled pupils don't need more authority, power and control from the grown-ups in their lives. Let's focus on giving these pupils what they need, what they either haven't had much or any of - yet. Let's provide them with sensitive, attuned care from grown-ups who can fill them up with everything they are going to need in order to be fully functioning members of both our schools communities and, in future, our society.

Over the years I have heard many different versions of 'golden principles', but here are my favourites:

a) Stay grounded and breathe, being mindful at all times

b) Have an open body language, a gentle but strong presence, and warm eyes

c) Connect with the pupil, so they feel noticed, known and heard

d) Give the pupil some respectful space but not too much: stay in close proximity

e) Commentate and wonder aloud rather than interrogating

I suspect that both staff and pupils would be more comfortable in a place where these core principles were at the heart of all our everyday comings and goings in school. There would be more 'felt safety'. If we feel safe, we don't need to use the defensive strategies that we learned to survive threat. If less defensive strategies are used, our schools become calmer and more peaceful places, where learning will more likely take place.

If that is happening, all of us (staff and pupils alike) will be freed up to be all we were intended to be; so we become able to function optimally and extend ourselves into the unknown, utilising our exploratory system to learn. Everyone feels more acknowledged, heard and known. Everyone experiences a greater sense of belonging.

It is incredible what these simple ideas might foster in a whole school community. What would it be like to try using these or coming up with your own and having them up for staff to work by? And how might you let your whole school community, including the pupils, their parents and governors know about your 'golden principles'? And what support might you and your staff need to maintain this approach, especially when times get tough?

Let's encourage staff to consider how we could 'do school differently' with both minds *and* hearts. This needs to be at the centre of our ethos. Troubled pupils see through 'the talk' and are **hypervigilant**, checking out that we mean what we say! They need to check this out as they have been alarmed too much in their short lives to date.

2 Increase relational contact

Following on from this it makes sense that we prioritise facilitating opportunities for face-to-face time with individual pupils. What they need to learn cannot be merely taught. They need to experience relationship. They need us to verbalise the unsaid. We need to give words to the states, sensations and feelings that are going on, not only in the individual pupil in front of us but also in the experience we are having together between us in the moment, plus a narrative of what is going on around us. This joint 'felt' experience needs our focus and attention. It is only as we make the links in 'real time' in our everyday life in school together that our troubled pupils will develop the capacity to become more integrated within themselves.

As **Senior Managers**, it is our ethical responsibility to choose to invest in people and relationship (rather than media) on behalf of these particular pupils. In some interesting research, Gregory & Weinstein (2004) found that adolescent perceptions of their connections with their teachers were the strongest predictor of academic growth in Maths from 8th to 12th grade. Long term, securely attached pupil-teacher relationships support learning. These relationships need **Senior Managers** to allocate Key Adults to pupils and to advocate for and facilitate the necessary time they need together.

3 Be well

So this leads us to reflect on how we can develop our current staff to be the best they can be, ensuring that we employ the right staff in the first instance. We have an ethical responsibility to be 'well' when working, especially amongst our most troubled pupils, our most vulnerable.

Most staff know this, and approach their work professionally at all times, '**containing**' difficult experiences until they are away from pupils. But we all know that regrettably, this is not true of everyone working in our schools. Ms X shouts. Mr Y can be super-tactless. Ms F gets bitingly sarcastic when he's dressing a student down. Ms P is a great teacher, but seems to have many home issues to deal with, and more problems with her classes than most. These are our colleagues, and in the pace of school life, we may wince but not make the time needed to address the issue.

But as a **Senior Manager**, you know that school is not the place for staff to be processing or rather 'acting out' their grief and difficulties from their own personal histories, including perhaps, insecure attachment: home or the therapy room is. We wouldn't expect a member of staff to stagger in with their arm hanging off after a horrible accident! And yet somehow we don't seem to pay too much attention when a member of staff is emotionally or socially upset or challenging in their behaviour - in other words, displaying dysregulated feelings and actions, that can quickly compromise the relationships with the pupils and other staff who come into contact with him or her.

Avoidance of what feels uncomfortable is often commonplace in the school context, and the role of the containing, supportive **Senior Manager** is to address these issues, to enable staff to be real and honest (by using attunement and acceptance, not judgement or evaluation), and to help them regain their own calm and groundedness. We need our staff to be aware of their own attachment history, how it has shaped them and made them who they are. They need to be aware of their vulnerabilities or 'shadows' too, so they can be mindful within their interactions with troubled pupils, and recognise when they need additional support or specialist input.

The more self-aware you are, and the more self-aware you can help your staff become, the more your staff team will be in a position to choose to engage in secure responses. Riley (2011) has developed a structured series of interviews to help teachers understand their emotional reactions, and to learn how to control them and how to function well without working on their own unresolved conflicts in the presence of individual pupils, within classroom contexts.

As a **Senior Manager** you need to know what type of support is available for staff in your local authority. In my authority, for example, counselling is available to employees, and I also offer supervision and support groups. If there isn't much going on where you are, why not consider getting together in your local cluster to set something up? There are some very creative partnerships out there. Go and explore, and be inspired.

4 Be both attachment aware *and* trauma informed

We need to be aware that most education staff will not have had much training in child development, attachment or neuroscience, if any (at this time of writing! I am hopeful however this will change, thanks to the work of the Consortium for Emotional Wellbeing in Schools). With this in mind, it's important that experienced practitioners, with rich experience of front-line work in education, are invited in to train staff up, not just in the theoretical underpinnings of this work but in how to relate and what to do as well.

There is a lot of interest now in attachment awareness from all kinds of organisations, but not so much interest in the impact of trauma that needs to be addressed too. Perhaps this is because our minds find it too hard to comprehend what can and does happen at the hands of fellow human beings. It can be overwhelming. At the very essence of trauma is powerlessness, and it seems that this powerlessness can reverberate through school systems unless we have those 'hard to reach' pupils 'all figured out'.

All human beings like to be in control - yes, even you and me! We are not just talking about troubled pupils here. However, something I've learned along the way (and need to be reminded of by my own supervisor at different intervals) is that often we have to manage and stay with uncertainty, rather than focussing too much on trying to 'take control' by fixing or rescuing another person. It is often hard to comprehend, but it is sometimes in the midst of discomfort or conflict that the most growth and recovery can take place. So much can happen in the process of being alongside one another. It is in the 'being' - and in the being together - that the adaption and recovery can occur. Our schools have become busy 'doing' places. So, let's remember the simple power of being.

As a teacher I find that hard, as my default position is to 'do' not 'be'. I have become stronger over the years, but I still have a long way to go, and mindfulness, for example can teach us a lot in this regard (*and see* p.73). Now, as a manager and trainer, I encourage all staff to 'stay with the uncomfortable feelings for a little longer than feels comfortable', and I recommend this to **Senior Managers** too (*and see* p.70)

5   Enable the pupil

I'm concerned sometimes to still hear of the preoccupation with pupils sitting up, being still and being quiet. We sometimes measure whether a school day has gone well using these criteria. Perhaps it is now time to remind each other that we are not in the classroom to silence a pupil, but rather to enable a pupil to be all they should have been first time around, to find their voice and their place in the world. We need to help them activate their compass, helping them find the right words for their experience, supported to do so within the relationships we create with them.

It may well be that our troubled pupils do need to move about. Trauma really unsettles the nervous system. It may well be that they need to protest. Trauma is unfair and wounds us to the core. It may well be that they behave badly for a while. Behaviour is all the communication they have until another human being takes the time to come alongside and truly understand, giving them attention and translating what they are trying to say, giving them the tool of words to express themselves well. Let's see one of our roles as discovering who this individual pupil in our care actually is. We need to leave behind our assumptions and embark on a journey of discovery. Quality time invested into relationship with these troubled pupils will be time well spent.

6 Include the anxious parent

At this time parents and carers have many reasons to be anxious, so please don't overlook or ignore them. Firstly, schools seem to be focussed more on academic results than on pupils moving forward developmentally. These days pupils and teachers alike are constantly being evaluated, and of course this also creates stress for parents, who wonder how their child will cope, and whether he or she is getting the right kind of support.

Secondly, many cuts are being made at this time. Parents and carers are meant to advocate for their child, and they may be worried about the impact of cuts on their child and want to discuss this with you. This is what a 'good enough' parent or carer should do. It's that advocacy that communicates to the child that they are safe and protected, even when their parents bring their concerns into school in ways that we may find challenging. We need to listen and work out how to go forward together.

Thirdly, some 'good enough' parents - for example adoptive parents and foster carers - have often had their own extensive experience and training in the realm of trauma. Because of this they are well aware that so many of their children's more complex and worrying needs are hidden. This brings a very complex dynamic into the classroom and school context, as it can mean that children who do in fact need particular types of support often go unnoticed, as they don't appear to staff to need anything (*see* p.33 *above*). They can present as quiet, easy children who don't behave badly at school. However, if you were to closely follow them over time you would see them 'unravel', becoming dysregulated and seemingly behaving 'out of character'. You would then realise that they actually have had and continue to have significant difficulties.

Some schools make the big mistake of naively assuming that the parents 'just need some parenting support', since the problems only seem to rear up at home. However, that still may not be what the children need. These children are often very fragmented in their sense of self. To be healthy, we need to have an integrated sense of self. We are doing these children (and their parents/carers and our education colleagues in later years) a disservice if we merely opt for the easy option of carrying on as usual without any additional support for children who are 'in hiding' in school. Time will tell. They will unravel at some point during their education journey. It is not possible to 'hold it together' indefinitely. Let's engage their parents and carers in understanding and working collaboratively with us on this, so that the likelihood of blame and **splitting** is reduced (*see* p.71) and the child or young person is better contained and supported by everyone.

Our ethical responsibility is to ensure that all children who have experienced relational trauma and loss in their early years have a Key Adult checking in with them on a regular basis and linking in with home. We need to gather up all the known pieces of the child or young person and integrate the pieces on their behalf. We can do this in all kinds of ways, but parts pictures (*see* (**IIH**), p.178) and parts language are especially helpful in this. Therapists trained in trauma recovery are also extremely helpful and can support this integration process, being specialists in this area.

Bringing it all together

As **Senior Manager**, how you promote the ethos I've outlined will go a long way towards making your school a **secure base**, not only for children with attachment difficulties and traumatic backgrounds, but for all your pupils, with all the positive outcomes in terms of learning and development that creates.

B THE SCHOOL ENVIRONMENT

For these particular pupils to flourish they need our schools to be relational communities. They need us to get back to the basics of being human. The fact is that we all do better and achieve more when we're connected to one another. So from an attachment aware perspective, how can we make the environment of our schools more relational, for all of us?

AN ATTACHMENT AWARE ENVIRONMENT

▷ Investing our scarce resources into people hours, not gadgets or accessories

▷ Having high expectations concerning staff giving sensitive, attuned care in their practice; recognising where troubled children are on the '**Circle of Security**®' at any given time (see *above* p.23, animation clip, **References**, and **Glossary**)

▷ Not being afraid of dependency, as we all need to negotiate this first before we can be truly *interdependent* (dependent and independent at the right times), a necessary developmental task.

▷ Saying sorry when we recognise we've made a mistake ourselves (see p.66)

▷ Realising that a change of staff will create feelings of loss. We need to be respectful of the grieving process that all pupils will go through, especially our troubled pupils (see p.69).

The Senior Manager in School

▷ Pressing the pause button in our busy, fast paced schools to allow for and encourage **reflective dialoguing**.

▷ Engendering fun! Playful approaches, for example Theraplay and PACE ways of being (*see* (**STL**)).

▷ Engaging in random acts of kindness for pupils, staff and families

▷ Facilitating different types of learning areas to meet all learning styles

Physical environment

▷ From the reception area onwards, having people around who are warm, open, kind, gentle and wise

▷ Saying hello/goodbye to individuals, using names at the beginning of the day, during the school day and at the end of the school day

▷ Creating areas of school for downtime, where processing can happen, for example safe spaces: and facilitating safety tours for pupils (*see* (**STL**))

▷ Increasing structure, supervision and interactions at breaktimes so our troubled pupils can succeed, (e.g. more staff, zoning playgrounds, lunch time clubs …)

▷ Facilitating sensory comfort around our schools so that all feel nourished and respected

Staff perspective

▷ Ensuring all staff have protected breaks

▷ Staggered breaks for staff so we have experienced staff on duty during breaktimes for pupils

▷ Quiet, sensory spaces for staff to recuperate at break times

▷ Staff having their own Key Adults checking in on them to see if they are OK

Parents' perspective

▷ Meeting parents/carers as soon as a Key Adult and Team Pupil are allocated so everyone can put names to faces

▷ Creating welcoming parent rooms in which staff can build quality connection with families rather than rushed conversations in corridors or formal, more corporate spaces

▷ Inviting parents/carers in to participate together with their children in different activities, for example gardening, baking, the arts

Wider community perspective

▷ Joining up with outdoor/active sensory based projects going on in the wider community such as drumming, allotment projects, forest school, junk modelling, playbuses, circus skills ...

▷ Taking children out into nearby cafés and parks

as appropriate to vary sensory breaks

▷ Valuing those involved in the pupil's lives (such as taxi drivers) by including them in Team Pupil

Ofsted perspective

▷ Encouraging governors and Ofsted inspectors to attend attachment aware and trauma informed training events

▷ Advocating for processes to be examined, rather than merely judging outcomes of pupils

▷ Lobbying for increased relational interventions within schools

C POLICY AND PRACTICE

Many schools are now creating policies for attachment awareness and trauma informed interventions. Over time, it may well become mandatory to do so as the essential nature of secure attachment relationships within a learning environment is increasingly recognised. Please see the pyramid overleaf for how these policies could be structured and integrated into school life. Such policies need to include expectations of Key Adults, expectations of Team Pupil and the expectations of the whole school community. The relationship with parents and carers will need to be mapped out too with general suggestions as to how to make the contact meaningful. The five pocket books in the **Attachment Aware School Series** are designed to assist you in this.

Attachment aware policies will need to outline how troubled pupils are going to be supported. How *discipline* will be used is especially important. Staff will also need to understand how to provide the necessary sequence of attention, so as to respect their pupils' biology (Perry, 2014): firstly, to *regulate*, then to *relate*, and finally to *reason*. Staff also need to understand the importance of *differentiation*, more familiar from curriculum delivery, in working from an attachment aware perspective.

The Senior Manager in School

Attachment aware support for those who are hurting in schools

(drawing on the Seguridad model used by TouchBase™ © theyellowkite.co.uk)

Complex trauma support

Trauma specialists involved, for developmental trauma assessment, planning & intervention Supervision for 'Team Pupil'

Specialist support as necessary

Relational trauma model of support

The need for a Key Adult: 'Team Pupil'. Individual plan. Differentiation of emotional & social tasks/expectations.

Relational support via Key Adult and 'Team Pupil'

Introduction to the impact of relational trauma & loss

Whole school training in attachment awareness including administration support, governors & so on. Stress regulation vs behaviour management. Attachment awareness policy. Differentiated behaviour/dignity policy.

Whole school foundation for all pupils

To discipline or not to discipline?

Some staff, and certainly some Senior Managers, may think that by offering our troubled pupils attachment aware and trauma informed interventions that we are actually taking the soft, easy option.

I say, *No way*! It is the most challenging option we can possibly choose. I say this having been involved in this kind of work for the last 15 years. It will take you completely out of your comfort zone. It will makes you re-think everything you have ever been taught. And a lot of the time, it will make you feel very uncomfortable as you straddle the two worlds of insecurity and security. But it is oh, so very worth it, when you observe troubled pupils actually settling to learn and remaining in their local schools surrounded by those staff most familiar to them.

So before we attend to the question of discipline, I think we do first need to ask ourselves what discipline is. I say this as we seem to have moved a long way from its original meaning. It actually comes from the Latin word *disciplina,* which means to teach (Siegel 2014). We know that in order for us to teach and for children to learn, they first need to be in the right state so they can 'switch on' their **social engagement system** and actually hear what we are saying. But if our troubled pupils are not in the 'right state,' in other words, in a state of calm or alert or at the lower end of alarm - then they will not be able to do this, and they won't actually be able to hear, since states characterised by high levels of alarm, threat, stress or dysregulation have been shown to shut down hearing mechanisms.

I don't know about you, but I can't see the point in talking for the sake of it (because of my own insecurity apart from anything else, as others may be watching!) if these troubled children can't actually hear me! If they move into alarm or worse still, fear, terror or overwhelm on my watch, then I need to be prepared for them to be switched off and engaged in defence strategies such as **fight/flight or freeze**, because they are now feeling threatened. The triggers for the alarm can either be internal or external. It's important to be aware that we won't always know what the trigger is but all of us can watch and learn the signs that indicate alarm.

So, I see it as our responsibility to first *regulate* (in other words to soothe, calm and stabilise the pupil), then *relate through connection*, and then finally find a way to *discuss reason with them* (Perry 2014). By doing this, in this order, I am respecting the biology of the troubled pupil in front of me, and supporting their development. Whether others understand or not, my first responsibility is to the pupil. This will mean that I will often delay my use of discipline until I have attended to the first two R's - those of Regulation and Relationship: so there may be a time lapse between them. I will only use the third R linked to discipline - Reason - when (and only when) the pupil is in the right state to make sense of the discipline, and to make good use of it for future times.

When we use reason within the work we need to keep our language succinct, not enter into lecture mode. We keep everything simple! *"You don't swear at me in class. That stops now."* We say short phrases like this in a firm but gentle and warm way, in a low tone so as to keep their thinking part - the pre-frontal cortex - online, and to prevent further alarm!

The discipline I use always involves *reunion* (in terms of my finding a way to re-connect, despite the rupture in our relationship) and *repair* (Golding 2013), in terms of my coming up with creative solutions that will put things back together in some way. For example - carrying out a random act of kindness for the child or adult the pupil has hurt. Or using glue or sellotape to attempt to mend something that has been broken.

My discipline will always involve my taking an active role too, not just the pupil. Whatever they need to make right, we will do it together. My core message to the pupil is always *"You are not alone now"*. These troubled pupils may have had to try and come up with attachment strategies on their own in the past, influenced by the threat of loss or trauma. However, on my watch, we work things out together.

The Senior Manager in School

Differentiation

So have you ever wondered why many children and young people in your schools seem to respond to your use of warnings and sanctions, remaining within your boundaries and learning socialisation quite quickly, whereas a minority seem to take no notice and even become worse in their behaviour presentation when these usual modification techniques are applied?

I'm going to give you two very different examples to illustrate the need for all staff to differentiate their approach to children from 'good enough' backgrounds and histories, from those whose experience falls far short of what we'd want for them. Just as you want your staff to differentiate for attainment, in order to facilitate academic progress, from an attachment aware perspective we must differentiate our behaviour policies and our approach to working with troubled pupils. The *communication* in their behaviour is key, and what we must be guided by. A one-size fits all approach will only lead to exclusions. If we are truly wanting inclusion, we need to differentiate to help all pupils settle to learn.

Take Lisa, for example. Lisa has experienced 'good enough' care and has lived with permanence. If she were to arrive late to my lesson or to start messing about, a firm look or a mild warning might support her to adapt her behaviour. She may feel slightly anxious, a little embarrassed maybe by my attention to her: but watch her recovery time. Before you know it she will have recovered and will be engaging well again. Why? Lisa has had the experience of a parental figure who has been physically and emotionally present, attentive, attuned and responsive to her needs most of the time while she was growing up. So she has a fairly robust sense of self - she knows where she begins and where she ends. She knows who she is. She knows that people make mistakes and she has just made a mistake.

She may even experience a touch of guilt - a sense of the other person, and her possible impact on their feelings - and so she can make amends. Her pre-frontal cortex is also functioning relatively well so she can reflect on and consider her actions. In effect she has had such **relational buffering** that she is now able to access her 'thinking part' at the drop of a hat. She has also had someone supporting her at times of big, overwhelming states, sensations and feelings. Because of this she now has the *internal* controls to manage *external* controls such as my limits and expectations. Lisa quickly settles back in and seems appropriate in her interactions, despite my having created a small amount of stress for her through correction.

However, take Daryl. Daryl has experienced **toxic stress** at the hands of his birth parents, where there was screaming, hitting, neglect and domestic violence in his early years. In order to survive all this, he learned adaptive responses, including **hypervigilance** and many other defence systems which have served him well. However, due to his experiences of **relational trauma** he has never learned who he was, what made him 'him'. He has a fragile sense of self filled up with toxic shame, maybe feels bad, flawed, maybe feels like he's a mistake. And because no-one supported him with his big states, sensations and feelings he has either no internal controls, or poor ones. In fact his nervous system is now 'fried', because of all it's been through; he feels uncomfortable and anxious most of the time.

With all this in mind, let's not be surprised if Daryl doesn't respond like Lisa. How can he? He still has to learn a robust sense of self. He still has to learn internal controls. Daryl has **developmental trauma** vulnerabilities which mean that of course he will not be ready yet for the whole school behavior policy. So why is it we expect him to fit into it? We wouldn't expect a pupil who hadn't yet negotiated number bonds to attempt algebra. *We would differentiate our curriculum*. So why do we not understand the urgent need to differentiate emotional and social tasks and expectations for some of our troubled pupils?

There are some pupils out there like Daryl who will need a Factfile drawn up and an Individual Development Plan (IDP) (*see* **STL** for templates). These pupils will need stepping stones to learn what is appropriate and healthy. They will need rich relational interventions so they can have reparative relational experiences. Then they will then need lots of

60

practice in order to become stronger in their sense of who they are and in their capacity to regulate. Yes, even to regulate the kind of slight stressors I described above.

If we don't differentiate we are going to continue to see increasing numbers of pupils 'breaking down' in front of us. Of course we don't call them 'breakdowns' in school. We usually interpret their coping mechanisms as the pupil being naughty, out of order or disprespectful, and so increase our power, authority and control in order to bring them into line. It may be possible to silence pupils for a while, through fearful submission: but do you really want to be encouraging submission when you know their histories? Wouldn't this leave them even more vulnerable to engaging with others who may then dominate them again? And I wonder what they might do when they have been shamed some more, when they already have a sense of being a mistake? Won't they act out that shame in some way, today, tomorrow or later on as they get older and stronger?

Now is the time to differentiate. We mustn't allow their stress or shame to increase on our watch. Toxic shame is costly for both the individuals, our schools and indeed our neighbourhoods (Music 2014) if our pupils continue to carry such tragically high levels.

EXERCISE I
THINKING ABOUT DISCIPLINE

- How were you disciplined as a child?
- If you are a parent, how do you discipline?
- As a **Senior Manager,** how do you usually discipline pupils, classes, the whole school?
- How do you discipline staff?
- How has your discipline changed over the years?
- How might your discipline change based on what you now know about troubled pupils and what they need?
- How might you apply what you now know to working with highly stressed staff who need to discipline their pupils?

EXERCISE 2

THINKING ABOUT DEPENDENCY

- Would you consider yourself capable of independence and dependence (interdependence)?
- How easy do you find it to be independent?
- How easy do you find it to be dependent on others?
- What did your parents encourage and when?
- What feelings does dependence in your pupils bring up for you?
- How might you apply what you know now to working with pupils who need to experience dependence?
- How might you explain the pupil's need to experience **relative dependency** in school to your staff? To the pupil's parents or carers? To Ofsted?

EXERCISE 3
THINKING ABOUT CONTROL

- What does it feel like for you to be in control?
- What does it feel like to not be in control?
- How will you manage the level of uncertainty involved in this kind of work amongst troubled pupils?
- How will you communicate with a pupil who has experienced helplessness and powerlessness in some way, because of what they have experienced in their earlier relationship with adults, but who is now trying to do all they can to maintain some kind of control?
- How will you communicate with a staff member or parent who says he or she feels out of control?
- How might you apply what you now know to working with issues of control?

EXERCISE 4

THINKING ABOUT TRUST

- Would you consider your childhood a happy one?
- If not how would you describe it?
- Did you trust your parents or carers?
- Do you find it easy to trust family and friends now?
- How will you manage being around a pupil who doesn't trust grown-ups?
- How will you ensure you don't take their possible rejection of you personally?
- How will you communicate with a staff member or parent who says he or she feels out of control?
- How will you support Key Adults if they get frustrated with their Key Pupils' lack of trust?
- How will you reinforce the pupils' sense of trust in your school community?
- How might you support the development of trust throughout your staff team, and wider school community?

EXERCISE 5
THINKING ABOUT PATIENCE

Do you have an impatient part? Most of us do somewhere. Well I do, at least, as my husband will be happy to tell you! Our troubled pupils will need our relentless care, requiring a lot of patience from those around them. The work will feel confusing and frustrating at times, especially when their progress is spikey and slow, not smooth and progressive as many other pupils' journeys might be. I have had to say sorry a lot in my role as an Attachment Support Teacher and therapist when I've somehow managed to let my impatient part express itself at the wrong time. But I've learned from those times, and to encourage you, I'm happy to say that I've found that these relational ruptures and most importantly, subsequent repair, often lead to deeper connection and big steps forward developmentally; so don't hold back on the repair front! A big dose of humility is often needed to do our work well.

- What tips you into presenting or expressing your impatient part?
- How do you know when you are starting to feel impatient?
- What strategies do you have for repair to your relationships when there is a rupture?

Bringing it all together

Don't forget that as a Senior Manager, what you do and what you say will provide a model for everyone else in your school community. Get some support if you feel you need input in any of the areas I've been highlighting.

D KEEPING THE MOMENTUM GOING

As this is long term support work, it is important that we prepare ourselves for the long haul. If we pay attention to staff care, their caregiving capacity and resilience will increase. It may cost financially initially, but the cost invested will reap healthy returns over the next two to three years. Sadly, if a school chooses to avoid addressing these issues, then the impact may, in the not too distant future, cost you, your staff and your pupils emotionally, socially, academically, physically, and yes, financially.

So please ask yourself the following questions to ensure you are prepared and ready.

a) If you have a Key Adult assigned to a pupil with a disorganised or reactive attachment style (see Geddes, 2006) in their presentation, do you have a back-up adult assigned too? It will take the intensity down if two members of staff can work closely together, sharing ideas and strategies as they go. It will also provide some of the support they need, as work with troubled pupils is the most challenging area to work in within the school context.

b) Who can be assigned to check in with the Key Adult at regular intervals? This is ideally going to be one of your Senior Management, maybe even yourself (see p.30). Key Adults need their own Key Adults! Someone who approaches the Key Adults, taking the initiative, not someone who waits for the KA to approach them. This person needs to be like a fellow traveller, encouraging, affirming and reminding the Key Adult of the journey the troubled pupil has made thus far.

c) Is there anyone who is clinically trained who could offer clinical supervision to support your staff, especially **Team Pupil** and your **Attachment Lead**? A counsellor, therapist or clinical psychologist who is attachment aware and trauma informed, who is linked in to your school? If not, start networking!

d) How can the Key Adult be connected in to other Key Adults in other schools? In my area we run support groups. Is this something that either your school, a cluster of schools or your education authority could facilitate? Our groups run half -termly over a minimum of a three year period, to parallel the type of support needed for each of our troubled pupils. Ideally these groups are off-site to facilitate **reflective dialoguing**, sometimes hard to do if you are on the school site aware that someone could call you out at any point!

e) Who will you refer to or check in with if the going gets tough? In my area we run support groups for **Senior Managers** too. It may be necessary to book in clinical supervision or a consultation at different points along the journey too. Think through your support plan for you (*and see p.75*).

f) What will you do if a Key Adult -
   ☐ goes off on long-term sick leave, or leaves permanently?
   ☐ says there is *"No point working with this one"*, *or* says they don't think they can take it anymore (verbally or physically)?

It's best to be as prepared as you can be. Here are my suggestions to get you started.

   ☐ *If a Key Adult goes off on long-term sick leave or leaves permanently*
   Facilitate some quality time and space to grieve together. Talk together. Acknowledge

and respect the different feelings around. Don't minimise or overlook the Key Pupil's loss. Give the child or young person the opportunity to experience a really good ending. Create a memory book of the work carried out with the pupil, outlining what the pupil was like or could do before and what they are like, can do now: the befores and afters. Reflect together on what the Key Adult has left them with in terms of parting gifts. Leave some pages blank to create new memories. Encourage cards to one another to say goodbye if possible. Encourage follow-up cards from the Key Adult if possible. Stagger the ending as much as possible to allow for the processing of this loss.

☐ *If the Key Adult wants to give up*
Get alongside the member of staff in such a way that they feel acknowledged, supported and heard. You may well not agree with what he or she is saying (at least I hope you don't!).

However, it is important that you stay at first with the uncomfortable feelings created by listening to the Key Adult's experience for longer than may feel comfortable for you, and that you communicate acceptance of that member of staff's perspective. For whatever reason, they may be suffering from 'blocked care,' which is a reality for those who get close to those traumatised pupils (*see* Baylin & Hughes 2012, *and* (**STL**) p.324).

The easiest way to unblock this is to increase your care of the member of staff. They will soon be functioning well again if attended to with enough understanding, care and support, and may feel more relaxed and hopeful and willing to re-engage. However, if the Key Adult continues to feel as if they cannot go on, you may also need to consider bringing in a trauma specialist, as the Key Adult's experience may be reflecting wider issues for the pupil and should not be ignored.

g) Please be aware that **splitting** is a possibility in the school community and in the relationships between school and home and school and outside agencies. The nature of the trauma that the child brings into the school can often result in staff teams becoming split, or making 'them' the parents/outside agency - into the 'bad guys' - or vice versa - with blame flying around. It will therefore be important that you take the lead in drawing others' awareness to this and that you **contain** difficulties as soon as you sense what is happening. Awareness, respect for and acknowledgement of one another's experience will shift this dynamic. Please get external trauma informed support if it does not.

h) **Secondary stress** is a reality for everyone regardless of age, skill or experience. No-one is immune. Enabling permanency in school for these pupils (rather than 'fresh starts') will take strength, courage and energy and honesty from everyone, if it is to work, and care for those closest to the pupil. So it will be important that you take the lead in facilitating staff care, detailed below in the next and final section.

E FACILITATING STAFF CARE

Stress can affect diet, sleep, focus, memory and the capacity to care. It is important that you look out for these signs in yourself and in the staff you manage. You may notice an increase in impatience, a lowness of mood, absenteeism, staff going into 'doing' mode rather than feeling … What else do you think you might notice?

In addition to the professional support meetings I've been advocating throughout the book, let's consider what we could do to dampen and reduce stress in a preventative manner.

Oxytocin is a protective hormone produced by engaging in relationship, fun and playfulness (as well as other activities). So reflect on what you could facilitate weekly, half-termly and termly for your staff to up their levels of oxytocin. How could you invest in them relationally? Here are a few ideas:

ONCE A WEEK
Breakfast meets, check-ins, notes of encouragement, random acts of kindness

HALF TERMLY
re-grouping to share successes, support groups, Circle of Adults (Wilson & Newton 2006, *and* Inclusive Solutions *in* Useful Contacts)

TERMLY
Going for a coffee, a meal, a team building activity, pampering, going off site to enjoy a sensory day together

Mindfulness training for staff?

Mindfulness and other techniques that staff might find helpful for centring themselves, relaxing and dealing with stress can be provided during INSET days or twilight sessions, and a small sensory space made available for those who might want to practise.

The Senior Manager in School

Importance of staff knowing who to turn to for support

I hope this book within the **Attachment Aware School Series** has given you the confidence to know that you are the crucial person for the Key Adult and the whole of Team Pupil to turn to for support. As part of your repertoire, please also ensure you have knowledge of a good range of other resources available to support staff, both in and outside of school (*and see* p.68).

Importance of bringing in extra specialists for back-up

The Key Adult, other members of Team Pupil or the parents and carers of a particular pupil may alert you to the need for specialist trauma informed input. It helps if you already have a working relationship with more than one individual who can provide this back-up in advance of the need arising. Who is in your area, and what is the best way to access their support? (*and see* p.44)

Importance of the staff room as a secure base

As I mentioned on p.50, providing staff with places to retreat to is essential for this kind of high intensity work, for example sensory space, as well as a comfortable staff room where people can re-charge their batteries with colleagues. Where possible, staff may also welcome outside space for time out and relaxation.

Self-care for the Senior Manager

It's essential that you look after yourself aswell: as you know, we all follow those who lead by example. I was shocked recently to hear **Senior Managers** on my **Attachment Lead** course say that they didn't have a favourite pastime or hobby, as there was no time. We won't survive if we don't attend to our own needs and interests. How easily do our interests get stripped away in the name of hard work? Note to self here! We are in this for the long haul. We need our staff teams to also be in it for the long haul. Others are watching! What we do really matters.

WHAT DO YOU KNOW WORKS FOR YOU?

What was your last experience of feeling really relaxed? How did you achieve that?

- ☐ What could you do today to give yourself a break, however short?
- ☐ What could you do tomorrow that you'd really enjoy?
- ☐ What could you start to plan in for yourself on a regular basis that you know will refresh the parts that need to be reached?

Finally

We have a lot to do. We need to stand firm and grounded, quietly confident in what we know to be true. We will be questioned. We will be discouraged. Our proposals will be rejected. But as **Senior Managers** we have an ethical responsibility to act on what we know, and to lead in this area. I cannot promise it will be easy, but hopefully it will be only a matter of time and our collective effort before this knowledge and practice will become embedded within school. Remember the campaign to raise awareness around the autistic spectrum, and how much work is still needed on this even now? To support others in the area of difference and diversity takes time too, but my what an investment! For our communities and all our futures - together. Attachment matters. Let's simply keep going …

If this book has stirred something in you and you would like to extend your knowledge and skills, then do consider Theraplay Level 1 and DDP Level 1 training, as well as Attachment Lead training (www.atttachmentleadnetwork. net). Our schools will be better contexts in which to learn and teach if we get relationships back on the map, especially for those who have experienced disrupted connections.

Senior Managers play a significant part in the adaption and recovery of troubled pupils. Don't ever underestimate the role and the influence you have. Always remember that even if these pupils can't take in all that you're offering right now, one day they will remember … our pupils are absorbing everything we offer them, one way or another. Nothing goes unnoticed.

10 pieces of advice from experienced attachment aware Senior Managers (collated over 10 years)

"It's important to get everyone on board including the governors."

"Training, training, training!"

"Stand up for what you know to be right!"

"Choose staff well …"

"You will be tempted to take over relating as a Key Adult to the individual pupil from time to time, but hold your boundaries."

"The school environment is key. Ensure these pupils feel comfortable in their bodies whilst at school."

"Keep reading. Be one step ahead to inspire others."

"Remember all this takes time and when the going gets tough remember your successes, however small."

"Time how long it takes the pupil to recover from everyday, low level stressors at school as this will change over time. Recovery time reduces as the pupil learns security."

"Ensure you get support for you!"

The Senior Manager in School

RESOURCES for attachment aware work - some ideas to get you started:

GARDENING PLOT OUTSIDE SCHOOL

BLANKETS

BEANBAGS

SAFE SPACE/S ALLOCATION IN SCHOOL

SLIPPER SOCKS AND FLUFFY SOCKS

LAVA LAMP

FAIRY LIGHTS

INDOOR TENT

LOW LIGHT LAMPS

CUSHIONS

WATER BOTTLES WITH FURRY COVERS

Crunchy and chewy snacks such as carrots, apples, celery sticks, health bars

Water bottles that can be frozen

Tin foil

Water/gel timers

Toilet rolls

Hand grips

Smelly soaps

Straws

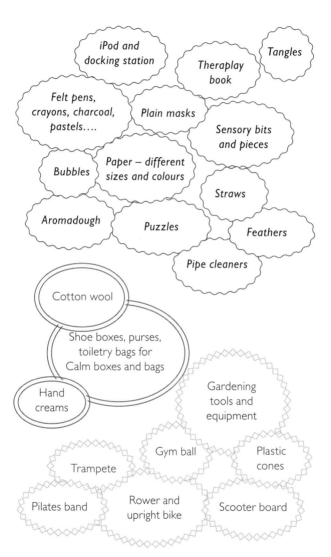

iPod and docking station

Theraplay book

Tangles

Felt pens, crayons, charcoal, pastels….

Plain masks

Sensory bits and pieces

Bubbles

Paper – different sizes and colours

Straws

Aromadough

Puzzles

Feathers

Pipe cleaners

Cotton wool

Shoe boxes, purses, toiletry bags for Calm boxes and bags

Hand creams

Gardening tools and equipment

Gym ball

Plastic cones

Trampete

Pilates band

Rower and upright bike

Scooter board

For a good supplier, please visit www.sensetoys.com

The Senior Manager in School

Glossary

Additional attachment figure This is the person
selected in school to get alongside a child with attachment
difficulties, here described as the **Key Adult**. This person could
be a teaching/learning assistant or teacher, or mentor. The task
is to relate to the child using strategies derived from attachment
and developmental principles. Their aim is to create a
relationship which will facilitate opportunities for second chance
learning, so that the child can have the experience of making
healthier attachments than previously. These experiences
encourage the development of neural connections in the brain,
which in turn leads to the development of conscience, cause-
and-effect thinking, logic and empathy.

Attachment history A child's history of significant
relationships and the security, or lack of security, safety, or
lack of safety, of those relationships with parents, wider family,
carers or adopters. It may also include other significant
individuals including teachers or even pets. Any type of
trauma and loss is especially important to note, even if a loss
had been deemed to be in the best interest of the child (for
example, loss of contact with an abusive parent): as is any kind

of extraordinary stress experienced. We need to know what they have lived through from pregnancy onwards, if there has been any kind of potential disruption to the usual bonding/ attachment process.

Attachment Lead An Attachment Lead is an appointed and trained member of staff in the school who seeks to lead the way in attachment awareness and trauma informed interventions and embed them into policy on behalf of troubled pupils. This is usually a member of support staff on the ground leading through practice with individual pupils, and a member of Senior Management leading through advocacy and strategic action amongst the whole school community. See www.attachmentleadnetwork.net for more information on the training required.

Attachment system An innate urge within humans (and other mammals) that impels us to seek promixity to and relationship with others. Attachment serves two important functions: a protective function and a secure base effect. It is in our interest to stay close to another person, especially when we are very young, defenceless and vulnerable. Staying close can keep us safe. It is also in our interest to have someone to act as our **secure base**. If we have a secure base, we are then freed up to set off out of our comfort zone into the unfamiliar, the unknown, into unchartered territory - the world is ours to be curious and learn about. We can do this knowing that we can return to our secure base before venturing off again.

Our secure base gives us the confidence we need in order to take the risks required in learning. Our attachment system (of neural connections and hormone release leading to attachment seeking behaviour) is activated if we experience anxiety.

Blocked care According to Hughes & Baylin (2012), when a child or adolescent continually rejects care and nurture from an adult, the brain systems that support empathy within the adult begin to close down as a protective response. The adult can feel frustrated, irritated, hopeless, rejecting or numb. They may continue to provide care, from a position of 'duty', but find it difficult or impossible to relate to the child from the loving and open engaged stance necessary for authentic and healing relationship (**STL** p.324).

Circle of Security® The Circle of Security® is a relationship based early intervention programme designed to enhance attachment security between parents and children. Decades of university-based research have confirmed that secure children exhibit increased empathy, greater self-esteem, better relationships with parents and peers, enhanced school readiness, and an increased capacity to handle emotions more effectively when compared with children who are not secure. The Circle of Security® intervention and the graphic designed around it are intended to help caregivers increase their awareness of their children's needs and whether their own responses meet those needs. With increased awareness, parents can expand their moment-to-moment parenting choices where needed. In this shift from mind-blindness to seeing what is hidden in plain sight lies the potential to break the stranglehold of problematic attachment patterns, passed from one generation to the next, that can compromise healthy relationships throughout a child's life span. (*With thanks to Jenny Peters and Glen Cooper*)

Containment When a baby is distressed or dysregulated, she needs repeated experiences of her parent or carer being 'bigger, stronger, wiser and kinder' (**Circle of Security®**) to help to 'hold' her feelings and experience and make sense of what is happening, until she is able to do this for herself. Similarly, adult individuals and teams need **Senior Managers** who can create containing environments to support their work containing children who have experienced relational trauma.

Developmental Trauma A term used by Van der Kolk (2014) and many other attachment aware and trauma informed practitioners to describe a child's experiences of repeated or prolonged trauma through neglect, abuse, abandonment, violence, loss, parental substance misuse or addiction. Developmental trauma implies that the child's developing brain will have been impacted, with negative effects on the development of their executive functions, motor skills, and capacity to self-regulate, communicate and relate. Left unattended at home and/or in school, the effects of developmental trauma are likely to persist into adulthood and have profound effects on every aspect of the individual's life.

Disrupted relationships/connections Relationships
and connections that have been disrupted or compromised for
the individual child through having early experiences of loss,
abuse, neglect, trauma, domestic violence, or parental substance
abuse or mental ill health. Disruption isn't necessarily intentional
(although it can be) but can come about due to circumstance:
for example, medical complications at birth, having a mother
who becomes unwell after birth … the ordinary development
of brain connections may have been disrupted if these
experiences happen at certain crucial times, or for prolonged
periods. Disruptions often compromise or disrupt trust. There
are many children in our care who have experienced intimacy
betrayals at the hands of their own birth parents. The deep
distrust that has been created out of relational experience
is then often projected onto other adults, regardless of their
intentions or motives. We can in fact get caught up in their
time-warp, experiencing the distress, grief and rage intended for
someone else, in another time and place.

Exploratory system An innate urge within humans
(and other mammals) that impels us to explore, experiment,
play, and thereby learn. The exploratory system (of neural
connections and hormone release leading to exploratory
behaviour) is activated or reaches its full potential when the
attachment system is well attended to. If the attachment
system is not attended to, the exploratory system (which is
needed for learning) will be impeded by ongoing anxiety.

The Senior Manager in School

Fight/flight/freeze response The range of responses we produce in relation to threat or perceived threat. Physiological, emotional and cognitive effects are triggered by the release of stress hormones. Each individual's most likely pattern of response is experience dependent. The pattern can be modified over time.

Hypervigilance A subliminal rapid-reaction mammalian defence developed in response to repeated or continual traumatic experience. The individual becomes wired for a state of high alert at all times to any potential danger in the environment, thus 'primed for threat'. He or she may view or interpret events, words or actions as dangerous which others around them view as innocent or innocuous.

Insecure attachment This indicates a level of insecurity that interferes with the child's ability to relate in a healthy or appropriate way to other people. Such insecurity arose from early uncertainties about the reliability of his or her parent or primary carer. We can observe too much dependence or too much independence in his response to his needs and the satisfaction of those needs. There are traditionally three main types of insecure attachment, sometimes described as avoidant, ambivalent and disorganised.

Reflective dialoguing Reflecting on experience, feelings, thoughts and patterns within a safe relationship with another person, in the interest of receiving support and gentle challenge to make new connections for deeper understanding.

Regulatory system If we have received consistent and sufficient regulatory experiences ourselves, through being attuned to and received by calming and soothing others, especially in our early years, then we are more able to internalise what becomes our own regulatory system (internal and external tools and strategies) to help us self-regulate at times of stress. If, however, we haven't had appropriate calming and soothing, at the right time, then our regulatory systems can be over-active and we can end up becoming dysregulated very frequently, even for everyday ordinary stressors. This is why many of our pupils need so much help with regulation.

Relational buffering Rich relational connection serves a protective function. It provides protection from the full impact of stress. It prevents stress from becoming toxic and damaging us. Those who have experienced relational poverty/withdrawal or trauma are very vulnerable and fragile in the midst of everyday ordinary stressors, as well as extraordinary **toxic stress**. This puts them at further risk.

Many of the pupils in our care who have experienced significant **relational trauma** and loss had to manage big overwhelming states, sensations and feelings on their own. Because this occurred when their developing nervous systems were very fragile, they have learned to rely on their feeling brain, and primitive limbic system in relation to stressors that come their way.

The Senior Manager in School

If we can now stand in the gap and give these pupils the sensitive, attuned care that they didn't have or didn't have enough of in their early years, then we are in effect providing them with the relational buffering they need in order to interrupt the impulsivity that occurs by using the emotional brain in isolation. We can in effect become like 'external brains', lending them our thinking brain to inhibit impulsivity, until they can manage for themselves. Check out the 'handbrain model' on Youtube, by Daniel Siegel.

Relational trauma Trauma experienced by the child on a repeated basis within the context of relationship (often from within early attachments) eg abuse, neglect, violence, intrusion, loss, abandonment and so on. The child may well have experienced overwhelm, powerlessness and terror in the process. The child may well now be completely confused as to the role and purpose of adults, having experienced such overwhelm in their care. It is not surprising therefore that coming into contact with us is going to mean them moving into pseudo-independent states, however caring we may try to be.

Relative dependency This term describes what we may be able to facilitate in schools, in order to give a child who has experienced early relational trauma and loss an opportunity for learning, trust and security through the relationship with a consistent adult who offers sensitive care: in this case, the Key Adult.

Safe space   A protected area/space or room full of sensory comfort to support a pupil either to upregulate or downregulate dependent on their state. This space is not used as an area for relational withdrawal or isolation but of time with the Key Adult. There is no expectation there will be talking; the best use of the area is to 'be together'. However both adult and pupil may engage in sensory activites, theraplay and PACE. The Key Adult learns the pupil and knows what is needed.

Secondary stress When an individual has experienced profound trauma, those working and living with them are likely to experience stress within their relationships and contact. This stress is a physiological and psychological reality, and those affected will need to seek their own support to help manage it.

Secure attachment This indicates a healthy and appropriate style of relating to other people. An interplay of dependence and independence is observed in response to needs and the satisfaction of those needs, as well as empathy for and generosity towards others.

Secure base A term used by Sir John Bowlby to describe what a 'significant other' (eg. a parent/carer at home, or a Key Adult in school) can become if he or she provides 'good enough' care for a child. It is from this base that a child can become free to explore and engage with the learning process in school. Equally a room with supportive colleagues can provide a 'secure base' for staff (see **attachment system**).

The Senior Manager in School

Social Engagement System Described by Stephen Porges (*please see* (**STL**) p. 80) as the open and engaged state achieved when an individual feels safe, and from which the individual will invite communication, understanding and joint interest in the immediate situation with another person.

Splitting When a child presents with a pattern of disorganised and insecure attachment, the adults around him or her may, in response to the strong feelings stirred up by the child's behaviour and responses, become polarised in their view of him or her and each other. Blame and division can easily develop. Team Pupil and the wider system around the child need to find support so that this 'splitting' can be resolved in the interests of the child and of preserving best working practices and relationships.

Toxic stress We all experience ordinary stressors in life. However if a child with a fragile and developing nervous system experiences extraordinary stressors, for example at the hands of his or her own parents, over a period of time, then the child can move into overwhelm. This overwhelm, which can include being flooded with high levels of stress hormones for significant periods, can put undue pressure on the developing body and brain, heart and mind, meaning that their natural development and functioning may become disrupted. This may lead to the state described as 'developmental vulnerability', or trauma.

References

Aspden, K.L. (2015) *Help! I've got an alarm bell going off in my head! How panic, anxiety and stress affect your body* London: Jessica Kingsley Publishers

Belsky, J., Vandell, D.L., Burchinal, M., Clarke-Stewart, K.A., McCartney, K., Owen, M.P. & The NICHD Early Child Care Research Network (2007) Are There Long-Term Effects of Early Child Care? *Child Development* Vol 78, (2) pp.681-701

Bombèr, L.M. (2007) *Inside I'm Hurting: Practical strategies for supporting children with attachment difficulties in schools* London: Worth Publishing

Bombèr, L.M. (2009) Survival of the fittest: teenagers finding their way through the labyrinth of transitions in schools *in*, Perry, A. (Ed.) *Teenagers and Attachment: Helping adolescents engage with life and learning* London: Worth Publishing

Bombèr, L.M. (2011) *What About Me? Inclusive strategies to support pupils with attachment difficulties make it through the school day* London: Worth Publishing

The Senior Manager in School

Bombèr, L.M. & Hughes, D. (2013) *Settling to Learn: Why relationships matter in schools* London: Worth Publishing

Booth, P. & Jernberg, A. (2010) *Theraplay: Helping parents and children build better relationships through attachment based play* New York: John Wiley & Sons

Brown, B. (2012) *Daring Greatly: How the courage to be vulnerable transforms the way we live, love, parent and lead* London: Penguin Books Ltd

Brown, B. (2010) *Ted Talk on Vulnerability* https://www.ted.com/talks/brene_brown_on_vulnerability?language=en

Cameron, C., Connelly, G. & Jackson, S. (2015) *Educating Children and Young People in Care* London: Jessica Kingsley

Circle of Security youtube clip https://www.youtube.com/watch?v=F6DhnbgRAOo

Clarke, J. & Dawson, C. (1998) *Growing Up Again* Minnesota, USA: Hazelden

Cozolino, L. (2013) *The Social Neuroscience of Education: Optimizing attachment and learning in the classroom* New York: WW Norton

Cozolino, L. (2014) *The Neuroscience of Human Relationships: A practical guide for the inner journey* New York: WW Norton

Forbes, H. (2011) *Overwhelm* - Beyond Consequences: Parenting Solutions Youtube v=X9zLKSoYOaO

Forbes, H. (2012) *Help for Billy: A Beyond Consequences approach to helping challenging children in the classroom* Beyond Consequences Institute, LLC. beyondconsequences.com

Geddes, H. (2006) *Attachment in the Classroom* London: Worth Publishing

Golding, K. (2013) *Nurturing Attachments Training Resource* London: Jessica Kingsley

Golding, K., Fain, J., Frost, A., Mills, C., Worrall, H., Roberts, N., Durant, E. & Templeton, S. (2012) *Observing Children with Attachment Difficulties in School: A tool for identifying and supporting emotional and social difficulties in children* London: Jessica Kingsley

Golding, K. & Hughes, D. (2012) *Creating Loving Attachments* London: Jessica Kingsley

Greenhalgh, P. (1994) *Emotional Growth & Learning* London: Routledge

Gregory, A. & Weinstein, R.S. (2004) Connection and Regulation at Home and in School: Predicting growth in achievement for adolescents *Journal of Adolescent Research* July, Vol 19 (4) pp.405-427

Hughes, D. (2004) *Facilitating Developmental Attachment: The road to emotional recovery and behavioural change in foster and adopted children* Maryland, USA: Aronson Inc

Hughes, D. (2009) *Principles of Attachment-Focused Parenting: Effective strategies to care for children* London: WW Norton

The Senior Manager in School

Hughes, D. (2013) *8 Keys to Building your Best Relationships*
New York: WW Norton

Hughes, D. & Baylin, J. (2012) *Brain-Based Parenting:*
The neuroscience of caregiving for healthy attachment
New York: WW Norton

Mate, G. (2013) *Attachment and Brain Development*
YouTube/v=UbiWLLYSZhc

Music, G. (2011) *Nurturing Natures: Attachment and*
children's emotional, sociocultural and brain development
Hove: Psychology Press

Music, G. (2014) *The Good Life: Well-being and the new science*
of altruism, selfishness and immorality
Hove, UK: Routledge

Olson, K. (2014) *The Invisible Classroom: Relationships,*
neuroscience & mindfulness in school New York: WW
Norton

Perry, B. (1999) *Memories of Fear: How the brain stores and*
retrieves physiologic states, feelings, behaviours and thoughts
from traumatic events Academy version, The Child
Trauma Academy Houston, Texas https://childtrauma.
org/wp-content/uploads/2014/12/Memories_of_Fear_
Perry.pdf

Perry, B. (2010) *Born for Love: Why empathy is essential and*
endangered New York: Harper Collins Publishers

Perry, B. (2014) *Brain Development and Learning*
Columbus Metropolitan Club, Youtube/DXdBFFph2QQ

Powell, B., Cooper, G., Hoffman, K. & Marvin, R. (2013)
*The Circle of Security Intervention: Enhancing attachment in
early parent-child relationships* New York: Guildford Press

Riley, P. (2011) *Attachment Theory and the Teacher-Student
Relationship: A practical guide for teachers, teacher
educators and school leaders* Oxon: Routledge

Siegel, D. (1999) *The Developing Mind*
New York: The Guildford Press

Siegel, D. & Bryson, T.P. (2012) *The Whole Brain Child: 12
proven strategies to nurture your child's developing mind*
London: Robinson

Siegel, D. & Bryson, T.P. (2014) *No-Drama Discipline:
The whole brain way to calm the chaos and nurture your
child's developing mind* Australia & UK: Scribe

Siegel, D.J. & Bryson, T.P. (2015) *Connect and Redirect
Refrigerator Sheet* http://www.drdansiegel.com/pdf/
Refrigerator%20Sheet--NDD.pdf

Sunderland, M. (2006) *The Science of Parenting: Practical
guidance on sleep, crying, play and building emotional
well-being for life* London: Dorling Kindersley

Sunderland, M. (2015) *Conversations that Matter: Talking
with children and teenagers in ways that help* Derbyshire,
UK: Worth Publishing

Taransaud, D. (2011) *You Think I'm Evil: Practical strategies
for working with aggressive and rebellious adolescents*
London: Worth Publishing

The Senior Manager in School

Thierry, B. (2015) *Teaching the Child on the Trauma Continuum* Surrey: Grosvenor House Publishing Ltd

Van der Kolk, B. (2014) *The Body Keeps the Score: Brain, mind and body in the healing of trauma* New York, US: Viking

Wetz, J. (2009) *Urban Village Schools: Putting relationships at the heart of secondary school organisation and design UK:* Calouste Gulbenkian Foundation

Wilson, D. & Newton, C. (2006) *Circle of Adults: A team approach to problem solving around challenging behaviour and emotional needs* Nottingham: Inclusive solutions

Wilson, P. The Blob Trees pipwilson.com / blobtree.com

Useful contacts

Attachment Lead Network	attachmentleadnetwork.net
B.A.S.E.® Babywatching UK	base-babywatching-uk.org
Beyond Consequences	beyondconsequences.com
Caspari Foundation	caspari.org.uk
Centre for Child Mental Health	childmentalhealthcentre.org
The Centre for Emotional Development	emotionaldevelopment.co.uk
Child Trauma Academy	childtrauma.org
Circle of Security website	circleofsecurity.net
Consortium for Emotional Wellbeing in Schools	jameswetz3@gmail.com
Dyadic Development Psychotherapy UK	ddpnetwork.org/uk
Heart Math	heartmath.com

The Senior Manager in School

Inclusive Solutions	inclusive-solutions.com
Institute for Arts in Therapy and Education London	artspsychotherapy.org
Institute for Recovery from Childhood Trauma	irct.org.uk
Nurture Group Network	nurturegroups.org
Theraplay	theraplay.org